A World Remembered

BOOKS BY T. ALAN BROUGHTON

NOVELS

Hob's Daughter, Morrow, 1984
The Horsemaster, Dutton, 1981
Winter Journey, Dutton, 1980; Fawcett, 1981
A Family Gathering, Dutton, 1977; Fawcett, 1979

SHORT STORIES

Suicidal Tendencies, Center for Literary Publishing and University Press of Colorado, 2003

POETRY

The Origin of Green, Carnegie Mellon University Press, 2001
In The Country of Elegies, Carnegie Mellon University Press, 1995
Preparing to be Happy, Carnegie Mellon University Press, 1988
Dreams Before Sleep, Carnegie Mellon University Press, 1982
Far From Home, Carnegie Mellon University Press, 1979
In the Face of Descent, Carnegie Mellon University Press, 1975

LIMITED EDITIONS (POETRY)

The Others We Are, Northeast/Juniper Press, 1979
Adam's Dream, Northeast/Juniper Press, 1975

LIMITED EDITIONS (SHORT STORY)

The Jesse Tree, Northeast/Juniper Press, 1975

A WORLD REMEMBERED

Poems by T. Alan Broughton

Carnegie Mellon University Press
Pittsburgh 2010

ACKNOWLEDGMENTS

Poems in this collection have appeared in the following publications:

The Antioch Review, Ascent, Beloit Poetry Journal, Blue Unicorn, Burlington Free Press, Cimarron Review, The Connecticut Poetry Review, Epoch, 5 a.m., Gettysburg Review, Green Mountains Review, Hotel Amerika, Hunger Mountain, The Literary Review, Margie, Mid-American Review, The Midwest Quarterly, 05401, Onion River Review, The Pinch, Poem, Poetry Daily, Prairie Schooner, Seneca Review, Sewanee Review, Southern Humanities Review, The Southern Review, The Texas Review, Tulane Review, Valparaiso Poetry Review, Visions-International

"Ballad of the Comely Woman," *Beloit Poetry Journal*, was published in *The Best American Poetry: 2002* (Robert Creeley, editor).

"The Kiss," "Anniversary," and "The Return of Strangers," first published in the *Sewanee Review*, vol. 116, no. 4, fall 2008. Copyright 2008 by T. Alan Broughton

"Refuge," first published in the *Sewanee Review*, vol. 114, no.2, spring 2006. Copyright by T. Alan Broughton

Book design by Laura Willey

The publication of this book is made possible by a grant from the Pennsylvania Council on the Arts.

PENNSYLVANIA
COUNCIL
ON THE

ARTS

Library of Congress Control Number 2009930161
ISBN 978-0-88748-517-6

10   9   8   7   6   5   4   3   2   1

CONTENTS

V. Leave-Taking

In Memory of
Annie Leigh Camm Hobson Broughton
1908–2005

I. Discoveries

A WORLD REMEMBERED

. . . as if on a winter's night you sit feasting with your ealdormen and thegns, a single sparrow should fly swiftly into the hall, and coming in at one door, instantly fly out through another. . . . Somewhat like this appears the life of man; but of what follows or what went before, we are utterly ignorant.
—Bede, *Ecclesiastical History*

But what if the bird flies from fields
through the doorway, the shade of the hall
and into high rafters, pauses to nest,
to feed its young, then takes wing again
in dusky heights of the loft, past
timbers, the hanging bats, toward
light at the other end, exit
from its brief stay here
where men have feasted and sung
and lain down to sleep on their robes,

and flutters into a wall
it cannot see? Like the sparrow
in my garage on Monday, taking refuge
in the dim cave while thunder raged.
It woke to the shadow of man, flew
toward light, beat wings and beak
on the vision of green and shade,
and the glass did not break.

Sometimes the soul stands pressed to a place
it can see through, face and both palms against
the undiminished light, naming distant
leaves and fruits it thinks it knew—
but cannot go beyond.

REMEMBRANCE

Was it ripe figs split glistening on the plate
in sunlight, or the way her bare hips rounded
in the shadow of a tree? Did the body
run and run through open fields
until he rolled in high grass and lay
waiting for light to reveal
some meaning for green bending above him?

Was there a time when he turned again
in the room where only moonlight touched
the silver of her sleeping cheeks, his hands
about to tangle in the shadow of her hair?

Over the body of the world he has known
he hovers no less than ever, although he wears
time like a tightening glove that shrinks
each day against knuckle and wrist.

Into the patterned shade of desires
alluring as they ever were he wanders—
hands open, breathing light—
through the dreams of a young man
in an old man's body.

DISCOVERIES

We are circling Saturn in its rings. Last year
I watched our pet machine clamber the rim
of a ditch on Mars. Tonight I hear dogs argue
with each other through open windows.
What do they say? *I'm here, you're there.*
Where is the moon? I watch a tyrant
thousands of miles away rage and blink,
showing how deep his ignorance of what
he really did lies buried. Beyond the planet
knowledge is never cheap, but here
it costs in pain and the slow process
of discovery. They tell me Neolithic men,
constructed like myself, found refuge
in fermentation. Yeasts break down
juice that we in our groping lift and taste
and take with us into the night, hoping
it carries enough of the sun that grapes
absorbed to light us onto the slope
of another day where maybe
what we learn is what we need.

HOW POETRY NEARLY DIED

After a poem ridiculing the new regime was posted on a government
building, orders were issued to kill all those capable of writing poetry,
and some 3,000 people perished as a result.
—Ebrey, *The Cambridge Illustrated History of China*

After the poets were killed, birds tried
to compensate and sang until they fell.
Too tired to fly, they littered the parks.
Stars winked out one by one, knowing
they'd never be compared to eyes again.
Leaves, roots and rocks looked alike,
and even the breezes went limp,
no longer stroked by metaphors.
The Emperor decreed that language
was reserved for his proclamations,
but when he spoke he choked on ashes.
Young girls waited by their windows
in the evening until they forgot what
they were waiting for, and mothers
in gardens below put ears to ground
hoping to hear the earthworms sing.
Soon everyone wore brown, and wine
tasted like muddy water. Somewhere
beyond the last village, a boy confused
by the first leaf of fall drifting in wind
believed it could be a butterfly, imagined
the sound of butterfly and leaf in words,
and all the blind in the cities, stumbling
into light and rainbows, could see again.

HANDYMAN

We noticed him when he came to town
only because dogs barked—itinerant,
sack on his back, ready to do whatever
jobs we needed done. He'd been to lands
we'd never heard of or believed were only
in stories—which he told well in breaks
between chores when we brought him cider
or a slab of bread. But soon the stories were more
than the work, needed by us, so that we pointed
at piles of leaves or downed limbs but said,
"Come in, I've just baked pie, sit down,"
and he'd begin. "Yes," he told the widow
waiting years for her son's return, "I heard
four months ago he fathered two sons,"
and then told of the war the boy fought in,
how it was lost, or told our preacher
how his daughter, taken as a witch,
was burned, afterwards found innocent,
now worshipped as a saint. Toward the end
of summer when he announced he'd leave,
we began to talk together, curious to learn
that what he'd told was always what we wanted
most to hear, even if the news was sad.
Each tale brought clarity to places of doubt,
light to a darkening landscape. Finally we sent
a posse into woods where he camped,
wanted to haul him back to the square,
ask why he'd tricked us with his lies.
Gone, of course. I tell you we went back
to our homes and had some weeks of looking
down when we passed each other on the street.
Then one by one, we talked, wondered why
we'd needed so much to live in his land

of 'once upon a time'—our land, we decided,
more than raked lawns and tended trees,
than the way light fell on a kitchen chair
and made it seem empty as wind. "Best liars,"
my father said once, "believe their lies,"
and so we returned to tasks of waiting out
our lives, but knowing them better than we had
because he read us like a book aloud, we listened,
and saw dim shapes before we fell asleep.

WIDOW AT SUNDOWN

Voices of strangers at other tables,
of children and grandchildren merge
with the wheeling mew of gulls.
Golden waves that lick moored boats
might make a watery Venice,
but this is a town of pebbled shores
fringed with hemlock and pine.
No mistaking his laugh, son
who leans to fill each glass,
or daughter's shrill cry
at her second husband's jokes.
Venice was before they were born.

What should a woman at eighty-six say
to loaves and fish and dewy bottles,
to hulls that thump a dock or waiter
who bends to take her order?
Once she smiled and said, "Choose,
love, I can't pronounce what I want."
Now lift chablis to globe the landscape
in amber, transmute it to poles in canals,
warm hand on the nape of her neck.

Her son pours, asks, "Enough?"
What do they know of *enough*
while generations chatter into dusk
or sleep is a night of mosaics,
furtive with incarnations?

Better let them think a still face covers
a placid mind—not this miracle, flash
of heat from the world of a rented bed,
ceiling that sparkles with broken light.

ACQUAINTANCE

After the ice storm I noticed hedges
in front of your house were bent to earth.
The next day all but a few were broken,
wood as raw as deep gashes in arms.

A week later when ice was only
transparent memory, scene viewed
in an Easter egg, your hedge was untouched
and path to your door still blocked.

Perhaps you went elsewhere this winter,
south to a warm courtyard with table
and chilled white wine, not far
from the obdurate murmur of breaking surf.

Surely you won't be there alone,
no more than neglected litter of storms
means you are ill or stilled by grief.
Is this why I do not dare to call?

I imagine your return and the day
I will pass, finding you with brush hook
thwacking the last debris into sticks
that you pile near the curb for hauling.

I'll call across the street to you.
You'll wave impatiently. Too much
to do, too little light before dusk.

CATECHISM

Did your mother lie down in the footprint of a god
and pray that her womb be filled?
She and my father lay in a bed they bought
and searched for their own delight.

Did she walk into fields, mouth wide in song,
praising the clutch of a dark bird's furious treading?
My father's sperm beat upstream against all odds,
driven by their blind need to swim.

Were you swaddled, then abandoned in field
or marsh, your mouth gagged?
At night when I woke howling from acid in my belly,
she held me to her weary body and sang.

When you lay naked in a wintry field, did beasts
breathe warmly on you or wolves give suck?
Fringed with lace, I kicked in the shade of a ginkgo,
pampered, bubbling at the spotted sky.

Did you slay with jawbone or sling, fall on your people's foes
with a shout that unhinged the stars?
I twisted in my heated flesh and cursed the home
that nurtured me, for I was sixteen and acned in soul.

When the dragon wilted to your thrust, did you bear
the golden woman home through long, chaste years?
My staff stood up and I walked where it divined,
smiling on all who brought succor.

And now as years bear down, do you sit enthroned,
dole sage words to your needy folk?
I gibber and flail as my fingers numb
and names of friends are listed stone by stone.

Then why are you here? What purpose impels your long descent?
I am here to touch water sliding over rock,
to lift my child from his crib when night bears down,
and then to wait in a white room wondering,
'What is that painting on the wall obscured by shadows?'

SONG ENDURES

Even the dead, grateful to stand
on Purgatory's shore, will pause
when song comes from the throat of one
who was a singer. Waves they crossed
beat on the shore, harmless; in the stern
their guardian cannot resist listening
to this song about their home, their lives
to its end before he gently chides
and shoos them on like a flock of doves.
Warm in a place of light more full,
more pure than any they knew, they recall
how a voice joined with words was always
more whole than any part they lived.
Adrift in the breeze that mingles sea
and shore, now they know the place
they left better than when they were there.

SCENE IN LATE MAY

In blurred wash of shade and sun
we sit and chat on a lawn.
Monet might have painted us
like flowers and flowers like us
and trees like shadowy clouds.

Dipping her finger in a cup,
the mother wets the lips of her child
whose lungs fill with air from a tube.
We speak of fine spring weather,
abundance of green, how friends
have passed the week. Not for long
can a body endure on air alone.

Finally we must sit and listen
to the rattle of a distant truck,
a voice from someone else's yard.
The speechless light surrounds us.

for Claire Margaret Schnell Barnaby, 1996-1998

PSALM

Was it squash soup with its flick of heat
from oil of pepper? Or buttery chardonnay
followed by well-aged claret? Say it was
cobbler, its peaches the last of the season,
arriving at market bruised but lush with juice.
No matter. We came in kicking the leaves,
nip of October in our lungs, ready to bring
whatever we were to the long table
garnished with favors for each guest.

We took what the gods and our hosts gave,
and leaning to hear each offered word,
we sensed the night and its causes around us,
grateful for lights in their chandeliers,
tales of cats and kids and our own buffoonery.
How easy to wear motley at a convention
of gentle fools.

                    Give us night after night
of glasses filled by generous motions of hands,
the helping boost for a mumbled story, eyes
meeting that do not glance away but pass
the spirit on and on till an hour when one
must rise for a task to be faced tomorrow,
evoking silence before the *missa est.*
Let us be ignorant that all at this table
can never be convened again.

                    And then riding
beside the one we chose long ago
to drive home with forever, give us
the known road winding down to a valley,
glint of stars like pinpoints on a map we marked

and hoped to travel before we knew where
we were going, before we came to that place
where a child has cancer, parents die
too soon no matter when, our angers lash
the ones we love. Help us remember how once
we found a house that sheltered us from grief.

for Skip and Mary Jane

GREAT BLUE HERON

I drive past him each day in the swamp where he stands
on one leg, hunched as if dreaming of his own form
the surface reflects. Often I nearly forget to turn left,
buy fish and wine, be home in time to cook and chill.
Today the bird stays with me, as if I am moving through
the heron's dream to share his sky or water—places
he will rise into on slow flapping wings or where
his long bill darts to catch unwary frogs. I've seen
his slate blue feathers lift him as dangling legs
fold back, I've seen him fly through the dying sun
and out again, entering night, entering my own sleep.
I only know this bird by a name we've wrapped him in,
and when I stand on my porch, fish in the broiler,
wine glass sweating against my palm, glint of sailboats
tacking home on dusky water, I try to imagine him
slowly descending to his nest, wise as he was
or ever will be, filling each moment with that moment's
act or silence, and the evening folds itself around me.

II. Telling Stories

THE BLIND MASSEUSE

After they name you, I ask you to strip.
Because my face is a wall, this is no threat,
and I can smile even if I've never seen
what muscles at the corners of lips can do.
Muscles, you see, are what I know—
the way they flow or bunch, coagulate
to ropes of tension or turn liquid
to the probe and stroke of fingers.

My fingers are not mere parts of hands.
They reach back to my wasted cells
where light should go, the place that reads
the forms light falls across. They use
that empty barn where I should have stored
what eyes receive and toss into hayricks
and lofts, piling in memory what dreams
can use. My knowledge is skins and lumps
of bone, cold iron of my bed frame
or a heated cup against the palms.

I hoard what I know from what I hear
as I follow sinew and bone that holds
each muscle in place when you speak
as if a hypnotist has called you back
to all you thought forgotten. I love the ways
you see, the snap of synapses, lightning
that alters your brain forever, even though
only sun glints on a glass of wine, inverting
the image of windows or a lover's face.

Tell me, tell me more, and I will loosen
every bind that holds you back.
You will walk out of this room as if blind

to all that conjures your nightmares,
as if you move through harshly lit angles and juts
of this world like water over stone,
your eyes blurred with the mucus of birth,
two hands lifting you upwards.

CROSSROADS

This is a place where three roads meet.
In a dream mostly forgotten, someone
told me not to be here—said only
that one road would be behind me,
not to be retraced. The other two
can take me to different towns and fates.
I've also forgotten where I'm going,
if I ever knew. If I'm running away,
why? Something dreadful was said,
but the words themselves are lost.
One road leads toward mountains
bruised purple by thundering clouds,
the other might go to sea if the coast
is near enough. No gulls here. I'm vexed
that no one has told me where to go
or why I stand here. A father should teach
a son these things before the journey
begins. I'm someone willing to learn.
Signs are too worn to read, and dead trees
give no shade. Distant dust foretells
a caravan of strangers. If polite they'll ask
me to join. I'd rather be on my own,
but I need to talk. Talking will help me know
where I am, where I may have been. I wish
my father had given me directions,
but I never knew him. Still, I'm furious
at that neglect. If these strangers are rude,
I'll not stand aside. I'll teach them a lesson.

CARNIVAL

Dusseldorf: February 26, 1854

When you have started, then the end comes,
as if of itself, to meet you.
—Robert Schumann

Stand by the rail and watch the revelers pass.
Pierrot jostles a Harlequin, Eusebius waltzes
a Coquette who soon will lift her skirts but never
drop her mask, and Butterflies pretend that Chopin
taught them how to fly. See how Pantalon greets
Colombine in a whirl of pleats and tassels,
and in the pause before the next surge comes,
you, Florestan, will turn to stare at the way
the river far below glistens and winks back
at you, flicking the city's lights against the stars.

First you will draw the wedding ring
from your finger, hold its empty circle
to your eye before you surrender it to water.
Even Clara's love can't change your destination.
They are coming again, voices, the hooting
of raucous horns, a rout that might be maenads
tearing the night limb from limb. You spread
your arms, mount the rail on trembling legs
become the prophet bird by leaping outward.
Like your future the river rises to meet you.

See how the fisherman you did not see
hunched in his boat near shore sculls
to retrieve you, drags you limp but breathing
from the pool. See how on shore the group
who carries you, pigs and devils and satyrs,

are greeted by a crowd eager to enjoy
this new charade, to follow your lax
and waxen body to the madhouse where,
muffling whatever music you might hear,
waits the coda of silence, the empty staves.

LEAVING A MARK

Power went out last night. Snap, and I'm left
in dark. TV dead, no way to trust
my feet on stairs, lumps of chairs and tables
crouching between me and bed. I waited,
watching candles walk in my neighbor's window.

That's when I got to thinking about what you said,
depressed as you were, how no one saw you because
your past was locked inside and you don't want
to talk about it. So don't. Why should they listen,
the young, sons or grandsons? Much too busy
making memories to waste an hour on ours.
Doesn't matter they rise so fresh in the mind
that I can still whistle a tune I've not heard sung
for fifty years. Who cares I was never famous,
no one knows I helped to pour concrete
for the Danville bridge or served as juror the year
we put away those crooks who torched their barns?

I know what you're afraid of—how when we go
it all goes with us. Yesterday I sat
on the porch, watched the neighbor's kids come home,
drop their books and stoop by fresh-poured pavement.
They made their marks with feet and hands, initials
carved with sticks. I stood and thought I'd shake
my cane, but why betray the fool I am?
They waved, picked up their books, went in to scribble.
On the middle span of the bridge, if you look hard,
you'll find my initials. But you would have to be
on your back floating down the river to see them.

LASCAUX, 1940

When earth collapsed and the dog fell through,
we stopped running, frozen on that ground
as if we might be swallowed too.
Wild olive writhing on the stony slope,
wind that stroked its leaves to silver
were no longer familiar. I was eight,
my brother twelve, our friend somewhere between.

But sun continued to cut its shadows
deep into rock and gully. When the dog
howled under our feet, we answered
and searched for a place to enter the cave.
We feared those narrow twists
where men and sheep could crawl
and never return. We followed the whimper,
spooked by our own breath magnified,
and did not dare to speak because
the passage changed our voices.

My brother touched a match to sticks
and gorse he'd plucked, and with that torch,
luring the limping dog to us, he also lit
the beasts on walls, some from our world—
horses, deer, and men reduced to simple lines.
But others were older than our thoughts,
shaggy and wild in their rolled eyes,
teeth flashing as they strained against
fierce winds. How could those frail figures
of our kind hold back the taut haunches,
restrain such creatures never to be herded?

We scrabbled out the next hole,
and for a while even sun could not

keep us from shivering. The dog limped,
more for sympathy than pain,
but I needed his warmth and carried him home
past upthrust faces of trusting cows
grazing the fence lines, past the field
where wheat in its docile rows was tan
with grain. When we told the men,
they made us show the place, and then began
visits from people who knew, meetings
that gave us three, for a moment, fame.

So many died before the war was gone,
all its bombs gathered finally into one
that hovered over the world for a while.
Now no one remembers us.
My brother died last year, our friend
is sixty-five and lives so far away
he never comes home. This is a time of peace
when people are always killing each other
somewhere else.

              I have been to those caves
once more before they closed them off
to all except the ones who know. In light
from floodlamps what I saw was not the same,
and I turned away to find them where still
they rise to claim me just before a dream
collapses into unremembered dark,
moving to the flickering torch.
Around them the pressure of rock
drags us deeper and deeper
into dense silence where they live.

WATER BABIES

I'll say they took you from me,
two or three, I never really saw—
stockings over faces, guns
they pointed at me, too scared.
I'll not tell how sun was bright
on the rippled lake, how many
options I had. Myself alone
in the car and you on the shore,
watching, calling out for me
to come back, but I sink
in my cabin of air, roll down
the window, accept the water.
Or myself alone on the shore
as you wait for the game to end,
expecting my face to swim
to the window, grinning,
telling you how to leave.
Or all of us there sharing
breaths as we drift to sleep
one by one as if on a couch
at home with the TV on.

Choice has always beat me
down till I have none.
Each of you came out of me
after nine months, each
gathered a body against my will,
and my will is a force
that drives me on and on.
What could I call the place
you fell into? Not love.
Is there love at all?

A breeze shakes water
and wrinkles it against the sun.
Such dazzle through a windshield
confuses. I fasten your belts.
You are safe, don't really know
me or my will—or is that
what they call a soul?
If I am your mother
I'm only a pod you burst from
after seed blew in. You squint
against the light, ask me
when I'm coming back.

Release the brake. Gravity
does the rest. You nestle
into water as if in my arms,
breasts in your mouths
too full of milk.
I'm only doing what I wish
someone had done to me.

REVISIONS

I stood at the top of the cut and called.
Hunched on the tracks, he smiled,
as if invisible in his crib, a game
we'd often played. *Come to me*, I yelled,
but already he could not hear.

In the first version I leap through brush,
over the fallen tree. We tumble into grass
and watch the wheels go by.

In the next one he walks toward me,
hands over his ears against the rush
and clatter of steel and rattling glass.
I run to meet him, and hand-in-hand
we stare up at passengers staring out.
He lifts his free hand, waves
at the flick of indifferent faces.

Or we are hidden in green.
Before the hiss on rails foretells the coming,
we have lain together in grass, spying
on the beast that can't leave its tracks,
his body tucked to my side,
the ground trembling beneath us.

In dreams we are not there
but on a trestle long abandoned,
staring at a rocky streambed far below.
As I turn he slips through my arms,
through lattices of ties, drifts down
becoming smaller and smaller,
arms raised toward me, until
he is a point of light, then gone.

Or worse, he lies in his new bed,
the one without rails, sleeping,
quietly breathing, but even if sunken beyond me
he is there, held in bounds
by tucked sheets, the rumpled pillow.

Nothing can change what happened.
We are staring at each other.
I cannot speak, the rush of sound
is on him even if I can't yet see
its origin. A million years of silence
have seized us. Galaxies pause
in their endless unwinding.
I see the dandelion he has plucked
and holds toward me. I see leaves
by the rail where it grew.

He has made a circle of yellow
by lifting it into air, away
from its roots, completed.

BARBERSHOP QUARTET

1. Death by Drowning

When my barber held Professor Wainwright's head
underwater in the sink, I want to know what
Wainwright was thinking—not what he felt.
I know the way hands after rubbing the scalp
in lathering strokes tightened on the nape,
pushed down, held the forehead firm against
porcelain. I'm sure Wainwright tried to lift
against the grip, his chest constricted.
Maybe he even opened his eyes, stung by soap,
bubbled a howl, then shut his mouth against
the influx of water. My barber tells me
Wainwright had once again praised Castro,
blamed all things on Battista and the CIA.
My barber's a man firm in his beliefs,
and they include loyalty to the flag
and detestation of all Commies. "I let him
breathe again," he said, "but I told him
the next time he stood up for that dolt
I wouldn't let him up or I'd nick his earlobes
with the scissors." No, I want those moments
before release when Wainwright knew
he didn't have the fulcrum to resist,
that his first deep breath was going to end
all those years of rattling on about the glories
of Shakespeare and Milton and Jonathan Swift.
What rose to the inner vision of his wincing eyes?
Did he wish he'd sported with Amaryllis in the shade
before he sank full fathom five? Was there one second
when the opaque suds parted and beyond the pearl-white
bowl he saw his father rising from the grave, a child
again, but furious in the light of his judgment?
He was released spluttering to the same old music

oiling the air from Nashville, other patrons
ignorantly waiting behind their *Field & Streams*,
to the blurred and stony face of the avenger
leaning to whisper in his ear. All I know is
what my barber told me because Wainwright
is long dead. I would have listened, shampoo
dribbling from my lips, and nodded, still bowed
to the ineluctable hands, the certainty of demise.

2. Fathers and Sons

My barber's getting old, only works half days.
But I'm retired and can come when he pleases.
To serve the other chair he brought on his son,
so now I sit and join the family when they let me.
I hear how Jay as a kid liked jumping
out of windows onto piles of cardboard boxes,
how he dreamed of being stuntman to the stars
and would have given his merit badge to meet
Bela Lugosi. Once I joked about how
his father, not there that morning, never aged,
must be drinking formaldehyde. "Don't laugh,"
Jay said, pausing with scissors near my eye,
and because I know his father's temper,
I winced. But it was only because he'd remembered
an interview he'd done for his radio show
with a man who knew Lugosi, confessed the star
had drinking problems, was even downing that chemical
before he died. I added another tall tale
to my anthology culled from Barber Shops, recalling
my childhood cuts with a man who lifted me
onto a board across the arms of the chair

and argued with my waiting father about Spinoza.
"Better to jump from windows," I said, and Jay
grinned, returned to snipping white locks
that I can't believe are mine. I didn't know
what to make of Spinoza or the words coming
to me in vowels still drenched in tones from Abruzzo.
When Jay was running the vacuum over my shoulders
he paused and into the silence said, "My Dad
thought we were nuts, my brothers and me.
But once when school closed early we caught him
diving from the third floor onto the stack
we'd left that morning. Just wanted to be sure
it was safe," he said. "Well, now I'm cutting hair."
I should have traded stories, said, 'Once I told
my professor father I'd never be a teacher
and then signed on to do it for forty years.'
But I figured he understood how we'd both
perched in a high window like all sons, taking in
the view of a distant hill and field, then jumped
just as far as our fathers taught us.

3. Running into Age

My barber ran marathons. For years I'd see him
on his own, churning through streets, his face
so absorbed in leg work that even my waving,
a honk, did not distract. Stuck in the mirror
where I see my own dull face watching scissors
work are clippings of his finishes and photos
of runners he admires. I've jogged since I was a kid,
told him so, and entered his world of decent people,
even if quirky because of the poems. He kept at it

till he was almost eighty, ambled through cancer
and chemo, sweated his way through dogs that bit,
drivers who tried to nudge him into the ditch,
the fastidious who objected when, on the nineteenth mile,
he didn't care where he pissed. He had good times
with companions and clocks, stayed younger
than any chemical could have provided. He even
talked me into one, and I ran it with my son
who finished ahead, thank God, since fathers
have to be careful about where they end up
in their children's minds. I ran through the streets
of my city for twenty-six point two long miles
and loved it, the way the crowds yelled at me
sweet things—that I was looking good,
was almost there. Where? Lord, I crossed the line
and was still able to drink and wipe my face and thank
the sun for hanging around. My barber quit
and I'm not liable to do it again, but we keep on
talking about hill work, sprints, the long runs alone
on a bright fall day when no one can tell you
you're a nut to keep pushing beyond the next
crossroad, the next, until you think you see
someplace you're going or might go or might have gone
if it weren't for the finish, not too far away.

4. Telling Stories

I substitute my barber's chair for the confessional,
babbling on about my life as if he could offer
absolution—not for separate vagaries or sins
but for the whole misguided system of my ways,
the chaotic contrail of a squib fizzling out.

Sometimes we swap these stories, but always mine
seem more injurious than his. I speak even though
I know someone the next day will hear what I've said,
even if not given in my name, because mostly
what my barber tells me are the lives of others
whose words fill his days as their locks drop
around him. At the end of each day out comes the broom.
The hair goes into a bin, the stories into his mind.
Was Homer a barber trimming the beards of
Agamemnon's grandson or Achilles' nephew?
I tell this near-stranger things I would not tell
my own wife, my son who once sat in Jay's chair
and listened as I spouted some tale of sad encounter
with a stripper in New Orleans, a joke really since
all I got from it was an empty wallet. I like to see
my barber laugh, I need to have him absorb the oddness
of my life and make me feel it's just like all the other
lives he's spent his days with. But midway through
I glanced into the mirror where my son, wrapped
in a shroud, was staring obliquely at my real face.
Did his hair stand on end to hear this man narrate a life
he thought he knew? And watching his wide eyes
I knew that I babbled on because I did not know
my own life any better than he, that tracking it down
with words was only another pastime, that some day
white hair would gather in his lap as his voice
invented his life and mine all over again,
and the barber laughs, and no one writes it down.

BALLAD OF THE COMELY WOMAN

As I walked out one day
I met on my path a woman
ugly as sin and walking a dog.
She stopped me and said, "Young man,

would you lie with me here
in this field where we're alone,
only my dog as companion?"
The dog went chasing a squirrel.

I placed a hand most gently
on her arm and said, "Old woman,
I've a wife and loving son
dearer to me than my life.

I could not betray such presences."
"Then," she said, "how like you this?"
and stepping to me her limbs grew slim,
her bare breasts brushed my chest.

O love, more than my hair stood on end,
and the grass looked so very green
I could not resist lying down
with her beneath me. "What if,"

I said between our kisses, "you change
again?" "I'm always the same," she said,
and therewith I was left with my face
in the sod and my own restless heart.

LYRICS FOR THE SAME OLD SONG

Your hair smelled like lemons,
the skin of your thighs was silk,
when you clutched my shoulders and moaned
I didn't hear tones of pain.

As a moon rose over the arbor,
we lay and stared at the leaves
that cut out ovals of darkness
and shivered in the breeze.

But we weren't cold, though naked,
and only moved as we breathed,
the slow in and out that stirred
an arm against an arm.

Somewhere a dog began howling,
you asked if the sundial could tell
the time of night from shadows
the moon cast over its stone.

You didn't want an answer,
I didn't want to speak,
we knew the whole thing was over
and time wasn't on our minds

except in ways it would be
for maybe a month or two
and then only years later
in lemons and shadows and night.

BALLAD OF THE USUAL BLUES

I could have walked to the moon,
I could have lifted the house,
but instead I turned off the lights
and pretended you were here.

I gave away money and jewels,
I burned all the poems I wrote,
or at least I imagined so
rather than going to bed

where the same moon so far away
turned sheets to banks of snow
and the house settled down on its stones
with the weight of my petrified heart.

Yes, I even saw that shape
of the typical valentine
as if you'd plucked it out
and called it anorthosite.

What's the point of being so glum
or thinking of all I can't do?
I'll stop thinking of you all night
or thinking of thinking of thought.

I'm standing at the window,
I'm naked as water and air,
but I haven't a claim to stake there,
no kinship with wind or weather.

I lay out the days of our love,
the nights when darkness was friendly,
like cards on a living room table
in a stalled game of solitaire.

ONE NIGHT

Avoiding your wife we snatched our times
before we reached that room
on your desk or mine or the back seat of cars,
accepting love's contortions.

A bed big enough to fly far away,
a shower like waterfalls
in Hawaii, and even the TV on
to hear the rest of the world

bombing and boring and selling itself
around us as we played.
I tried to imagine night after night
of hearing you breathe beside me.

But at dawn I woke to spilled Kahlua,
you standing at plate glass
watching an empty highway. I saw
how flesh hung loose from your waist.

You turned a stranger's face to stare
at a body that withered around me
as if all the digging hour after hour
had only sheared our roots.

We checked out at eight, drove and joked
as wet flakes fell around us,
talked about Monday's clients and hopes.
One wiper didn't work.

On the sidewalk near home I stood and waved,
your signal winked at me
and a small tree in the clench of pavement,
bent by April snow.

AFTER THE WEDDING

"I'm tired," she says, "let's skip the reception,"
so they shake some hands and leave.
Rain falls straight, blurring the green
of August. She keeps her face

turned to fields. Too often they've been
to funerals there—friends
and a child. Near their house she cries,
"Look how the river's up."

Through the glass she wipes with her palm
he sees the swollen rush.
"Headache," she says, "just the damp,"
and goes early to bed.

Light is dim all afternoon,
rain on shingles a mat
of relentless sound until at dusk,
silence. He looks through the web

of needles and boughs to clouds roiling
beyond the pines. He hears
the river hurling itself on banks,
heaving flotsam at boulders.

He thinks she can sleep because the church
is a place that matters to her,
where words are sung, "Losses," she says
"healed by voices together"

that only leave him numb. She'll sleep
and rise as if consoled.
Late at night, the only way
he knows to fill the space

left by the death of their son is to trace
the river from its source.
From clouds furled on rocky peaks
water fills a pond,

then overflows and twists through granite
fissures, banks, the brook
and gorges on tributaries—down
a cliff face to the lake,

a stream that slows in a spreading marsh
and beaver pond, but tilts
again, gouging the steepest clefts.
On nights like this it rips

at banks, rolling more stones to the valley,
surging through fields and roads.
Far to the south it meets a sea,
but that is much too distant.

Here, the storm has passed. In the dark
he stares at points of stars,
the milky way still but unwinding.
Was that her voice? When he leans

he hears only her steady breathing.
In bed he asks the river
to enter his dreams, bear him away
to the place where waters are one,

but he knows he will wake to discover again
that grief is a smooth stone
swallowed into the clenching fist
but always there when it opens.

CROSSING

and we make for a shore that is nowhere.
—Pindar

We thought we would go there together
in our boat made of stone.
The sun came up, the sun went down,
and we saw no reason to doubt.

When the moon was shining brightly,
my mother sang to the stars,
and my sister stared at the water
and told me never to cry.

I went deep under the decks
to rooms where the paintings hung
of mothers and fathers before ours
and eyes that never closed.

"Sing," I said to my father,
"or speak in an unknown tongue,"
but he only stared at horizons
and placed one hand on my head.

He was the first to leave us.
We woke and searched the deck
but boards were dry and cracking,
and he left no sign.

My mother slowly went mad,
or at least she fell into silence
and stared and stared at the hands in her lap
and would not say our names.

One night my sister called me
out of my bed at dawn,
and her voice was cursing the bitter waves,
and the waves were all I saw.

I heard all three of them singing
when waves rode over the hull,
and then last night the silence
was nothing I understood.

We won't go there together—
no, we won't go there at all—
the boat will keep going forever,
and I'll never touch the shore.

III. Later Than You Think

FINDING THE FALLS

Dear Ted: I didn't mean to sound so sour,
so unwilling to listen to your 'good news.'
I think you've always seen the brighter side.
I didn't mean we shouldn't walk the moon
or risk making fools of ourselves in space. Or die.
We do it, feet on the ground, day after day.
Why not in orbit or descent? But I'm torn
too often by the tug of war that comes
from ignorance and knowing what we know.
I'm no good without facts, can't understand
how they could say this morning on the news
that telescopes have shown us time beginning,
let us know we're always spreading out,
and how what we see is less than what we can't.
Maybe I'm afraid that soon they'll look
so far in cells they'll see us before birth,
attach some chip to send back news from death.
When you'd left I napped till dinner, watched
the sun hiding itself behind the mountains
—yes, I know we spin to make the dark,
but I don't see it that way. Over my wine
I remembered that summer fifty years ago
when young Jim Russ and I (well, I suppose
he's not much younger than I am now) found
Fairy Ladder Falls, lost since Colvin
named it, described how they could never forget
the sight. And soon it lived up to its name,
something elves had shown to taunt surveyors.

All that summer it rained day after day,
and Jim and I, lugging our axes and saw,
tired of clearing trails, slogging through muck,
blades that glanced off bark before they bit.

One day, alone, I heard a rush of water
I'd never heard before, then thought I saw
a slash of white at the valley's head. Next day,
we laid our tools by the trail and bushwhacked down
to the stream, clambered along the bank. I guess
no one'd thought to take the fork to the left,
—the other in low water must have been
more promising—because in half an hour
we were there. The sun came out, the water
took that light and tumbled it down the steps
of rock, breaking it into colors, spreading it
into tongues so bright that I could see only
the burning falls when I looked away. And it stayed
with me into night, after we'd stood there
silent for an hour then scrambled back
to the path, still saying nothing till I said,
"I guess we've found it after all these years."
Jim and his uncle went back later that week
to be sure, then claimed they'd found it. Never mind.
You don't make a penny off such things, and what
I wanted was what I'd seen. Never went back.

Here's why. I couldn't decide if I was happy
or sad to know that it was really there.
Since I was a kid I'd seen it in my mind,
read what Colvin said, heard others talk
as if it was a mystery they loved.
One day I'm sure they'll make a trail to it,
and hikers will sit near the spray or skinny dip
in the small pool at its base. When I stood there,
then turned my back, I wanted to say to Jim,
'Swear you didn't see this. Swear to me now
we only imagined what we saw.' But no,

it doesn't work that way. I'm even glad
tonight that I can see it in my mind,
so why shouldn't anyone? I guess I'm saying
don't show me where I come from, where I'm going.
I need to have the sun spin and rise
from this dark where I can hear the bullfrogs
boom along the side of the pond, the owl
barking down the ridge, so I can take
some night one last, deep breath and praise again
the miracle of light before I can't.

ORIGINS OF DESIRE

I first saw you in a garden
where we walked after school.
Under trees you reached for fruit
but were too small to touch
the lowest branches. I turned
to pull my mother's hand
and then you were gone.
Or were you hiding behind
cherries or plums beyond?

When we were tall enough
to pluck the fruit,
I found you there alone,
but I was too shy.
Passing through shade and light,
you paused to look back,
and I wished the apple you bit
could be the one still clutched
in both of my hands.

PORT OF DEPARTURE

Nothing, so long as I am in my senses,
would I match with the joy a friend may bring.
—Horace

When I came to Brindisi, Horace,
we traveled by rattling trains, not mules
and boats or weary feet. During that year
in Rome, our Emperor mined a distant harbor,
sent his daughters to buy jewels and scarves
at Via Condotti on Christmas Eve. You rejoiced
in the presence of friends, among them Virgil
who did not know he would one day guide
Dante to the gates of Paradise. We arrived
no less weary at the dark port where lights
from moored boats trailed on oily waters,
and workers waited to lug their battered bags
on deck, bound for Patras, then scattering
over the bony hills to home, if anyone waited.

Brindisi, Horace, was your destination. For us,
escaping the plucking hands of gypsies
and crumbling stones of aqueducts and tombs
was only a stage toward the next retreat—
down the shattered spine of Greece, pitching
through waves from rocky isle to isle until ahead
was only blue Aegean and our wrecked lives apart.
Ours was a backwards journey from paradise
to the purging of love in fluttering candles
at dawn, hell of divorce. I swear, Horace,
I had no better friend until we called it love.

SCHOOL DAYS

School was the smell of a lunchbox
never cleaned, or sneakers
tossed to the back of a locker.
But we were clean and combed
till recess and the first tussle,
a race downhill to the tree
that served as jungle gym.
Someone's football arced
above us, then it was time
again to lean and pretend
that long division made sense
of our lives, spelling was crucial
to moments before we fell
into sleep and dreams that merged
and transformed faces of friends,
teachers, the eyes of parents.
No smells, no one demanding
sense, and the twisted grammar
of our ways was as private as lives
of adults who guarded the doors.

SMALL VOYAGES

Down to a dock where fog clung flat
to the lake and hollow knocking was pressed
close by dense air as we dragged
canoes from their racks, out we thrust
into water so still only my hand
deep on the paddle could tell it from air.
In the bow I was first to enter unknown
worlds of silence, my blind face leaning
into a place that might have been sleep
but for the shiver of flesh, alert,
the swirling rifts we made until light
pulled aside chill gauze to reveal
we were only floating on water, staring
at ragged shapes of trees on shore,
the sudden rise of startled loons;
and slowly, pulling our weight with steady
strokes, we returned to a sun in its sky
and thought we remembered who we were.

THE FIGURE IN THE WINDOW

Like my father, I stand
at the table's end to teach
what I know of poems.
Through arched panes I see
distant views of a building
like my own but filled with doctors
naming the subtleties of veins,
the harmony of cells and nerves.
This week light is honed by fall
and shadows deepen.

Always the figure stood high
in the distant window, back
to me, white and severe.
I envied his composure.
With little dignity I confess
my love of some poet's dactyls,
wondering in lapses what
my father did when Dido ranted
at her flames or Turnus
took his fate in the guts.
How can we teach
the prosody of what we love?

Today I wore my specs
and plucked from his square of glass
the hanging bones, pale
anatomy of the dead.
My fellow teacher always keeps
his mandible in place,
yet mutely managing to say
Timor mortis conturbat me.

I let Keats rise slowly
from my lungs, dance
across my gesturing tongue
and into the soft-dying day.

KOREAN PASTORAL

Stranger in this land, I climbed
the cobbled path to visit Buddha
who sat in a cleft above the sea,
his stone face always greeting
the morning light, and at his feet
were flowers plucked and braided.
No one approached in silence
or bowed to his sandaled feet.
Children tumbled and shrieked
as if he were more friend or kin
come to this place to celebrate.

Tall and white-skinned, I was
good luck to touch, fingers
running across my shoulders
or feeling my elbows,
and when I walked back
to waiting buses, they held
my hands to make their circle
whole, and danced.

What luck could I bring them?
Already they owned the fortune
of laughter, the joyful touch
of fingertips as if they read love
in the Braille of my bones.
In town they led me to tables
strewn with small cups of wine
and cakes of rice and honey
sweet as the Buddha's flowers.

LATER THAN YOU THINK

1. When Instinct Becomes Thought

Knees bent, on the balls of your feet,
face your opponent. Grip the throat
of your racket with the left hand.
Now he has served, and the ball
is crossing the net. Identify the shot
as forehand, turn your shoulders
perpendicular to the net, weight
on your right foot, racket drawn back
and ready to move forward, transferring
your heft to the front foot, and, O yes,
keep your knees bent, your left arm
now relaxed and reaching out so
you can fling it away, bringing your hips
and shoulders into action, providing
the power of torque to your stroke,
and keep the racket moving up
and through, finishing high. Did I forget
to tell myself to start with its head
low? Yes, low to high, that's it.
See how easy a forehand is?
But isn't it odd that suddenly like all
things you did by instinct, now
you have to think through each step?
Here you are still standing on
the court, ball long past you, opponent
weary of waiting, gone home, lights
out, facility closed till dawn—you
with your racket high, your torso
still half-turned, the ball at rest
behind you—and maybe tomorrow
you can take a whack at a backhand.

2. Aches and Pains

First a muscle, then a tendon or two,
and what made that bruise on the heel
of your palm? It doesn't take much
pressure anymore—loosening muscles
are peaches, overripe. But that's what
they wrote, isn't it? *Ripeness is all.*
You know you're getting late
in the process when under the flesh
the girder of bone aches all by itself.
For relief, go to the cabinet, bewildered
by so many bottles. Did they breed
overnight? Surely you didn't buy them
one by one. Forgot your glasses, can't
read the labels, much less instructions.
Your teeth? Before you get the brush
to your mouth it flips through fingers,
extorts a groan as you lean to retrieve it.
You stand too fast and smack your head
on the cabinet you forgot to shut,
but the pain in your head is less daunting
than seeing the caricature of your face
in the mirror, gaunt and gouged
with erosions. Leave that fluorescence,
too much like the glare of a final room,
sink into your sagging chair near
the open window, breeze of the dark
summer night, and take a break
before you have to find some way
to lever yourself upright again
with petulant arms and legs.

3. Forgetfulness of Sleep

Between feet and hands is a distance greater
than that between the memory of making love
and its possibility. To tie the shoe you must sit
and bend over the shelf of bony knees, fingers
fumbling to find the end of a lace. How long
since you stood like a heron on one leg
and pulled up your trousers, how long since
you simply launched yourself down the stairs
despite the sudden pitch of space rather than
standing for a while to teach your foot to lift
and lower squarely on the next riser? Your wife
remembers better than you the place where
you put down your car keys—or do you suspect
her plan is keeping them out of your grasp
forever? I'm asking you too many questions,
and like myself you find it hard to hold
more than one at a time. Relax. It's early
afternoon. Without disgrace you can doze
over a book, if dozing is waking to a cricked
neck when someone calls, *Dinnertime.*

4. Inattention

I wonder if the reason that you listen hard
to someone's joke but can't stay with it
long enough to catch the punch line
is because you find yourself each day
in the middle of your own joke but
don't want to know how it ends—
because you can't imagine it will be
funny even if everyone else in the room

will have to find some way to laugh again.
Do names fade only seconds after
the introduction because you know at last
that no one can tell you what you really
need to know, just like all the books
and music and art failed to go beyond
and report back also? Dear friend,
here is the hardest moment of all.
Sitting in that sidewalk café, perhaps
in Rome for the last time, I saw you
sipping espresso, staring past tables,
and your head did not even turn
when that perfect shape of rounded
breasts and hips swung by on heels
that made her sway from neck to toe.
What could you possibly have seen
in a headless torso across the street
on cracked pedestal, name defaced?

5. And Finally Tonight

We have an interview with yourself, and here
in moments before we summarize the news
of the day you have a chance for final words,
impressions, the sort of review that might
one day be an obituary if we have a segment
left late in the hour. Speak. Reveal. Better this
than if a priest stood over your prostrate form
and intoned, the very one you avoided
for so many years. You are moving your lips.
Your eyes look out to us, to our light, my face
as I bend to listen. You recognize me now,

I guess—yourself in one of the stages
you imagined you were when you thought
you were, or dreams enabled you to believe
you held in a porous net some shape
of yourself that was not water. Quickly.
The credits must be shown. Only seconds
left, don't turn away. Isn't there some last
image? A tree where clinging locust shells
spreads a simple shade, a stone imbedded
with a point that might tell time, a voice
speaking your name in a room too far away.
That's it. On to our sponsors. But watch
the tape of your life played backwards.
Such fancy steps, so wonderful the ways
your gestures fold inward to the source.

WHAT LASTS

Men shoved cameos at us in streets
of Naples or alleys of Sorrento
where we walked against a cold wind
from the sea. The land, gouged by armies
tossing each other back and forth,
and faces incised with loss also rose
around us as if carved from obdurate
shell, claiming the right to persist.

I watched my mother peer
at brooches to divine their age,
the quality of craft. I held an oval
thrust in my hand. I was too young
to judge the profiles of women,
trees, or towns by small harbors.
They burned in my palm as if
the folded needle pinned them
to me forever. *Save me, save me,*
the eyes of each vendor pled.

Long after makers and buyer are gone
I hold one to my northern sun
that ricochets through empty rooms,
and I sink through pines fringing the sea,
laden lemon boughs leaning to soil
where ruined cities rise again to light.

IV. In a Time of Need

LAMENTATION IN A TIME OF NEED

Laudato si', mi Signore
—St. Francis of Assisi

I. Out of the Garden

I have not seen Saint Francis in his robes
walking this earth, feet bare, hand raised
in blessing. I have only stood in a garden
where flowers and shrubs and winding vines
surrounded his statue, stone bird in his palm.
Living wrens fluttered in arbors nearby,
the fountain at his feet splashed glints of light
across his ever-serene face. Buddha too
could hold still like this, eyes turned inward.

Francis, come walk with me past cranes,
past weary men napping, white with dust,
or dropped on ropes into new-formed caves
returning with empty arms. Teach me to sit
by a pilot, firm in his hate, steering passengers
into the maw of his own death, and to touch
his taut jaw as he turns to the shining wall.
I need to believe there is another peace than death,
another love than the bitter struggle to accept.

II. Brother Sun

In that brightest of fall days
sky seemed made for you,
Brother Sun, to fill with light.
We were the ones who brought night
into morning, rising smoke and dust

that shrouded thousands who died.
We stained the gentle air with wailing.

Always moving outward, rushing in flames
toward your extinction, you drag us
helpless in your wake, and yet each day
you give us hope of a new morning,
our pledge that what we have done badly
and cannot undo we will not do again.

You spare us the blast of your explosions,
send us only strokes that raise trees
and grass, defeat the hopeless dark,
and even remind us through your sister moon
that you are still there, enduring.

Tell us the fiery plunge, heat that melted
steel and stone was not what your making
was about. Even your indifference is better
than mortal hatred. You are not love
but can teach us to love with the warmth
that brings out leaves to shade the nest,
that helps us learn to sing.

III. Moon, Stars, and Wind

Peace is for us to keep or shatter
and what surrounds us cannot say more
than gestures of wordless stars
scattered across the sky, the calm, soft palm
of moonlight on our foreheads.
No matter what wind brings us

we are never diminished as now
when little remains to be buried,
when oblivion is what we have made
from some place so rank and dark
that as we walk in sorrow believing we see
the shapes of clouds, wind in the waving hay,
we still pull shadows around us
and stuff the singing mouths with ash.

Pray that in the rubble of our hearts we find
some fragment of song older than any
we have made so that each day we hear,
as if Bach or Mozart were performed
beyond the woods, a pulse in air.

IV. Mother Earth

Mother Earth, receive these stones and steel
bloodied as if they were our flesh,
take this scar we made on you
and where we built towers of shining glass
give us flowers, weeds, whatever is green and grows.

Mother Earth, who spins through night and day,
who travels with us in space too huge to know,
forgive how we cannot relinquish our need to kill.
Our books are filled with lamentation
since words were written down,
our songs slant into minor keys.

You have known your children longer
than they have known themselves,
and still you bring us forth and let us

lie in an open field with birdsong and sunlight.
I must believe you know some phrase we hear
only in our deepest dreams and cannot yet
bring to our mouths and then the air.

Let each stone and fragment of steel that we return to you
lie silent and deep, sinking into those places
we cannot see or know, beyond memory
of each smile or voice as singular as fingerprints
that were lost forever in that blind rush.

Gravity pulls us always to you.
But for a while we stand, we walk,
we watch for you in horizons rising from each dawn.
We look around us seeing fruit on the trees,
bending limbs, and wonder how
this ripeness can be ours when again and again
we bring back to you much heavier remains.

V. Father Death

I do not believe there is another life
than this—the cool brook rippling over
luminous stone, chilling my hand
when I plunge it deep in a quiet pool.
My childhood horror came in black and white—
gaunt faces in a camp, bodies stacked and naked,
mockeries of any human forms I knew.
Now death comes in colors radiant as Van Gogh's,
these blooms of fiery gas more like stars
or galaxies we photograph from space,
forming or dispersing forever.
Before another tower rises,

before the chain-link fences come down,
night after night will pass when even rubble
is gone. Cats will cross warily, old papers blow
in wind before snow falls, blurring shapes
in a landscape of memory, that place
where something was and never will be.

Father Death, without you we would not tend
this garden far away where the statue of a saint
is always praying. The stone bird in his hand,
the live one singing on his shoulder, the water
falling to rise again and play with light
are made for any who choose to open the gate,
pause in shade of cypress and yew.

For a moment there is wonder for these things
man gathered, maybe even that deeper silence
we call love held in this parenthesis of peace.

REFUGE

When sun was slanting through the trees
they met in the woods. Dawn
was safer than walking through fields at noon
when guns were firing at random.

He knew he'd be shot if they found him there—
by one side or the other—
and she came dressed in a brother's clothes,
her hair cut short and ragged.

They'd grown up together on neighboring farms
before the killing began,
had met in woods when the only fear
was having some hunter find them.

Now what point in making love?
They stretched out side by side,
and sometimes they whispered, sometimes lay
in the comfort of their breathing.

They heard the flutter of a hawk,
the rabbit's one, shrill cry;
she shuddered, and he stroked her hair
that only smelled the same.

Late afternoon the first bombs fell
somewhere near the village.
Earth shook, and one dead tree
dropped through windless air.

When light was all aslant again
they knew the dusk would come,
and he walked with her to the edge of the field,
watched her tread the furrows

until she passed a distant copse
and night turned from gray to black.

HISTORY OF A STREET

When we skipped down that street,
singing in the dark, what did we know
of Via Rasella or Ardeatina? Armies
had come and gone in marches
as old as layered stones, shards
of amphorae and busts. We sang
because we were ignorant and young.

She stood in the doorway and swung
the hips of her wide and shadowy form,
chanting she'd take us both for the price
of one. We stared across that line
between our innocence and her offer,
could not speak, and strutted off.
Who blamed her for throwing a stone?
We thought the only human failure
of that street was our sheepish own.
What other song could we have sung?

The killing site already had its plaque,
bones were reclaimed for consecration.
What song remains in Via Rasella
or on streets where men and boys
were seized, except the usual cry
of swifts building on high ledges,
women calling from windows?
When trucks were crammed with priests,
officials, boy of fourteen, assorted Jews,
someone howled a name, a dog barked
at rigid shadows on the walls.

That night we slipped past parents
in our homes to beds and dreams
of what we might have done.

RUNNING TOGETHER

I want the fox to help me forget.
He runs in panic, meters beyond me.
I stride through blue fall air, exult
in the surprise of his russet fur, the paws
and long tail dipped in black. A fence
tucked low to the ground keeps him with me.
He settles into a pace for the long haul,
and day surrounds us with fallen leaves.

Today I watched tall buildings collapse,
the burst of bloody orange, imagining
flames that hurl me from great heights.
So many stories calling out at once
are not a book we can read,
marking down chaos one page at a time.

How slowly those minutes pass, the fox
a red slash across remembered blasts.
He lopes in a blurred world of motion,
and we cannot retreat to a time when all that steel
stood firm, when someone was lifting a pen
to make order on the cluttered desk.

Run, fox, run. When the fence is gone
I will follow you into an open field
toward the woods beyond. I do not know
how to accept my species, so much stranger
than yours. No matter how I hate the brothers
who killed, kinsmen I would not want to claim,
they have hurled me once more into the pit
of failure, have made me stand witness
to the flawed and twisted wreckage of our brain.

The collapse is inward now, deep
into the rubble of mind. The fox will lose me
in the woods where he knows all turns
toward safety, the den where, panting,
he can hide. I will go home, play Bach,
try to believe that this is what our cells intend.

When cranes lift some chunk of stone,
no Lazarus will rise to our waiting hands,
startled by day, gathering words to tell us
what prayers he uttered in that underworld
of dark and dust and extinguishing moans.
I am at home and my fingers play only notes.
Sometimes debris above me shifts,
and I remember the dash across green,
cruel beauty of dead leaves, fox-fur stroking light.

MAN IN THE WOODS

*It is a basic principle in Jewish law that saving a life is of supreme,
paramount importance. It takes precedence over everything else,
whether you know him or not.*
—Zev Friedman, rabbi, Long Island, NY

*In Rafah, near the Gaza-Egypt border, an 18-year-old Palestinian
was shot in the head by Israeli gunfire after nightfall.*
—Associated Press

From hundreds of miles they came to search
our woods. Few of them knew him, but he
was theirs by faith, the deep descent to Moses,
Abraham, the rainbow of promise. He had left
his wife and wandered off the trail, into scrub
and hacker bush, toward the cliff-edge hidden
by moosewood and windfall. What burning sign
did he follow into the falling sun, the silent dusk?

Here at my desk piled with everything undone
I try to imagine whether fear gave him time
to sit, lost, waiting for deliverance as trees
tightened around him, breathless. The others
search because each man is a fragment
of all men's love, each who has come this far
deserves voices calling to him, the feet
in street shoes stumbling on roots and rocks.
Listen how his name changes in the ricochet
from granite, how even his wife's lament
is smothered in spruce and moss and tangled
fall of water. When he is found and carried home,
his body is the body of any man, his chance
for watching stars again as past as their light.

Although I have no faith I can name, no robes
for the rituals of doubt, I will join you.
Let's go into desert places whether through streets
or only the dry hiss of sand. Take with us the body
of this single man hunched in dawn,
no less worthy of our love when dead.

MOMENT OF SILENCE

This is the house where children died,
where gas leaked slowly up the stairs to fill
rooms where they slept, a hall where the dog
curled on its own bed and never woke.
These are the parents who came home late,
smelled nothing wrong, but staggered to the lawn
holding the remnants of their lives—lanky arms
and legs that dangled like puppets after the play.

This is the moon that shone all night, full
of reflected light. See how years later it rises
again above the trees and roof, again makes
shadows from whatever stands between itself
and earth. The rooms were stripped bare,
other occupants strew their chairs and toys,
drop clothes on scarred floors. We don't recall
their names, those of us old enough still
to wonder at the way even sorrow lapses,
fades when our homes are elsewhere.

But sometimes driving by, in a pale shudder
our breathing holds as if we can prevent
the coming of what we cannot hear or smell.

THE KISS

The door slid open, I lugged my bags
into the room where a crusher smashed glass
as one by one the woman fed it bottles.
Back to me and hands at her sides, someone
was watching, as still as if that shattering racket
pulled her back to childhood disasters, tumbler
in pieces on the floor, milk pooled at her feet.

"Sorry," the woman shrugged. "So many."
I said, "No hurry," glad to pause in my indifferent
rounds of stores and lines and pumping gas,
but when the other turned, older than both of us,
her broad face smiling, I thought I must know her
because the eyes were so sure of what they saw,
her voice so warm in her "Hello, hello"
when she leaned to kiss my cheek,
hand fluttering on the back of my neck.
I kissed her too, and the day was blessed
even if I could not raise her from shadows
of my mind. "Mother, Mother, that's enough."
The smile dimmed as if we'd let her down
again. "Sorry, Alzheimer's," the daughter said
groping deep in the soggy bag. Her mother
turned her back, leaving me hollow.

I wanted to stand beside her, rest my arm
on her shoulders while we watched the empties
of their daily lives recycle, wanted to lean
my head against hers and remember that kiss.
Must we suffer some flaw before we can smile
and kiss the stranger? Is love so hard it endures
without memory? They left me with my bottles,
and one by one I turned them into shards.

BEYOND THE GARDEN GATE

As you see, the sun is high and the heat is great, now is aught heard save the locusts in the olives; wherefore it would doubtless be folly to go anywhere just now.
—Bocaccio, *Decameron*

Yes, without doubt it is better here.
Jays swerve from the sky,
smears of blue. The dog at our feet
stretches in shade, ignores the squirrel
at the feeder's base. Cloudless, midday
repose in a green expanse of limbs and lawn
where drowsing is to weave
from shadow to light like a breeze.

Elsewhere the infant stares through flies,
calm, beyond hunger. Sirens approach
the place where blood already congeals
and mourning has begun. Tomorrow
you can read about the child with a rifle,
tomorrow raped women will testify
in ways that tell the future's history.

We'll tell stories when more than one
of us gathers here. The voice will carry us
for a while to old places with new names,
people vaguely familiar. See how they think
like us, lie down with each other,
sometimes when they shouldn't,
but only the puppets moan with love
given or lost. They can lift a plaster arm
at the end of a string and be more gay,
or sit as we might in another time,

plucking a lute, singing madrigals
through someone else's throat.

Stay here. Don't go beyond this gate
where they are dragging wagons to the pit
and there are not enough shovels to go around.

ON THE ROAD

In the old folks home for indigent women,
my uncle guided me down hallways
where warped linoleum snagged my shoes,
windows high in walls sucked light outwards
into a gray November sky. He ran the place
for the state, wanted to tell me changes
he'd make—all he needed was money.

Eager to hit the road with extended thumb,
I let his voice drift unheard until we stood
in a bathroom where he pointed at a tub.
"So deep she couldn't climb out, too weak
to turn off the water, hot only." Beyond
the window I saw a warehouse, bare tree
and bends of a pewter river.

My uncle was a good man who died
much later, "Of natural causes," they said,
if that's what it's called when your cells
run amok and eat your liver. I went home
after I stalled in New Orleans, never saw
that place again, never forgot rusty stains
on porcelain, echoing drip of one faucet.

RESTORATION

Dredged from a burial ground, what's left
of his aged body in stone is torso,
one leg and arm, a noseless face
with sunken eyes and down-turned mouth.
He would have leaned his weight on a cane
as he mourned his wife recumbent, dead,
but she is gone. Even his staff
is broken. What he depicts is how
the living felt about their dead,
the marble ending that waits for all.

If I stand close enough he stares
at me, but I'm not a missing spouse,
and I must leave to walk the streets
where a woman muffled in collared coat
might be staring beyond her stride
to a child she never had or lover
who will never unlock their door again.

Let me lean tonight on elbows
over a glass of cabernet,
see the reflection of your face
in a polished spoon. Candle flames
pulse with each breath of our passing words.
Let's conspire to make such fragments
come together when we lie down
in the ending of this day, complete.

V. Leave-Taking

HARROWING THE FIELD

My cousins sat me on the tractor.
"Make straight rows," they said.
Needing advice for what I'd never
done, I looked to my father.

"Drive on," my cousins yelled, but his glance
gave neither faith nor doubt.
I slipped the clutch, the engine leapt,
and I drove without looking back,

dragging bright wheels that slashed the soil,
gauging what time and grace
were mine before I had to turn.
I don't recall the rest.

But the day became this recurrent dream:
my lines slurring to curves
until I reach the central point
with no field left to plow.

I idle the tractor and stand to survey
the narrowing coils that mock
the pattern I planned, and then I walk
those furrows back that unwind

my way to where I began, but older
and no one there to listen.

SONG FOR SAMPSON

What did we do for Sampson our cat?
For years we opened cans for him,
we spread out feast after feast
of golden-fleshed salmon, fine bits
of chicken in thick broth, and he ate
both morning and night. Each day
after he scratched his litter box
we emptied whatever he dropped.
Our laps spread like grassy plains,
and he alone was the pride, sunshine
flowing around the slats of the house
that was his cage, spreading over him
like honey, and his fur grew warm.
At night we gave him whatever place
on our bed was without the kicking feet
of our dreams, creatures he could not see
or smell. Often he lay on the rise and fall
of our breasts, the tide of breathing
and slow slap of heart as we rowed
toward morning. We took from him
all propagation and its will, left him
uncertain why faint odors of a passing female
made him stretch and sniff as if he sensed
his own life embalmed in air, a pharaoh's soul.
And this is why he pissed on our shoes—
not out of anger but to help us carry him
with us wherever we walked in the wide
world he could not enter, spreading musk
of Sampson over the surface of earth,
until he became immortal as the darkness
we eased him into, leaving us blessed.

THE OLD ORCHARD

for Littleton Long

Apples hang ripe on his trees,
and surely light that falls between branches
      casting shadows of leaves
on the very green grass is almost the same
      light that fell there in other years.

At least you would have trouble
telling it from whatever the sun did before,
except for memories of what came between
and also the fact that the man who tends

the trees and apples and mows the grass
      has not taken the cover from the sign
that says Apples For Sale—Two Hundred Yards
because he has taken his memories and left us.

He will not climb the ladder that now lies on its side.
He will not gather bruised drops
      and sell them for cider,
nor will we stand in his yard,
      our bags of astrakhans and pearmains
leaning against our shins while we wait

maybe less for change than to talk when he returns,
which he won't do now or ever again.
                And sometime in late fall
when puddles near the porch have remained
frozen all day, when the moon itself seems iced
with a cold and indifferent blue of distance

we will pause walking home and hear the earth
beating a dull, random thump and thud
for each falling apple—rhythm of time-keeping
more like memory than time—

falling to the place where they will slowly
merge with soil, with roots
of the bent and propped and dying trees.

AN ENDING

Early fall, the clouds skim low and dark,
wind tears leaves and apples plummet. Frost
tonight will flatten the green that grew too late
in the garden. I'm old enough to know this happens
again and again. I do not grieve—why doubt
I'll see the same when summer ends next year?

If you still live in my mind where winds and cold
can numb, how explain your absence on the day
when I wake and fickle sun melts frost, pretends
this might be spring? No answer from where you are.
Fill the feeders so birds survive the winter;
seasons are for the living, not the dead.

for John Engels

LEAVE-TAKING

Rock

In the lake it rises just above the surface.
Summer waves lash the worn peak
always in touch with sun or stars;
in winter water holds still around it,
ice and snow shaped to its shape.
That is why Abenaki called it center
of the universe, last place the god stood.

Departure

Dusk, and a breeze from the far shore
carried scents of blossoming vines, resin
from fallen needles in forests spreading
up the valley to bare peaks. Fish leapt
in the calm lee of the rock, geese rose
and slanted to bays. The god stood
on the lake's stone center admiring
all he had made, longing to remain
by the spark and flash of water sprayed
with final light. He knew how deep
were silent waters, how by day or night
this world would be the only sign
of his coming. He made the rock to stand on,
fields ready to turn silver with dew in dawn,
and also those two figures on a distant cliff
staring at the falling sun, uncertain whether
its light was the same that struck the rock.
What were they doing with their arms—
waving farewell or pointing as if to explain
to each other what they saw? For a moment
wind and sun held still, the long lake

was unruffled, brooks did not flow.
Only their arms kept moving,
either pleading or trying to hold on,
and then the god was gone.

Locations

Or maybe the god did not leave.
Stand on that rock when the lake is frozen,
black with depth and booming
as layers shift with the turning hours.
Walk there because you want to leave shore
and its cares, mid-winter piles of old snow
crusted with grime of days. What you find
is silence except for hiss of a small wind
scudding against your legs or hollow moans
that travel the length of the lake. If the god
is still there in that thin air of zero,
dispersed as each flake of crystal forming
in bright sunlight, gathering into prisms
gone before the rainbow is complete,
then all you need to do is stand
in that one place and find some way
to open a prayer in the silence of your mind,
some fan or scroll depicting a gaunt maple
weighted with snow, white space surrounding.

Dispersion

We too know sorrow the god felt,
scattered into all creation—into the still
and brackish pool of some cedar grove

or larvae clinging to stones of the rushing brook,
the lichen indifferent to long, dry months.
Bend by the lake's edge on a day in fall
when death could not seem more remote,
when leaves blaze with fury and light,
so stubborn in their wrenching of air
that you wince and cannot breathe,
and at the height of such insistence
you recall you will have to leave all this
one day, will never again reach a hand
toward water streaked by wind. Still
you will stand there at dusk in the shadow
of the god's regret praising the last light,
praising the wide-winged heron
for its slowly descending flight.

for Joan Smith

GOING TO GLORY

Be careful what you say. The last words
of Isadora Duncan were, "My friends,
I go to glory"—right for a deathbed,
for heroine speaking even to critics
or cognoscenti who had watched her read
her solar plexus before moving.
Or not moving, since fans believed
all she had to do was stand
and the world around her danced.

What you say now might be the last
oozings of your ripe autumn, words
you wouldn't want to be remembered for
like "Damn it, why are these creases
still on my collar," or "Why is my coffee
always cold?" Out the door you go. Brakes
on the garbage truck have failed. You join
the other roadkill on your street.

Isadora, down to her last franc, pretended
she had the cash to buy a Bugatti,
and when the handsome driver arrived,
she flung her long red scarf around her neck,
said her final words to passersby
(friends knew better than to be there),
climbed in and tapped the driver's shoulder.
Gas, clutch out, scarf winding around
the wheel's spokes, and Isadora dead.

Each day I leave the house I cry, "I love you,"
to my wife, the dog, a watching cat,
whoever has the patience to hear me,
practicing even when the house is empty.

SHALL I COMPARE THEE?

According to early Icelandic law it was a serious offence to address a love poem to a woman, even an unmarried one.

Love prefers the least contact to the greatest distant joy.

If I loved the moon I would not praise
the varied light she casts from night to night,
nor tell her how much she fills the dark and somewhat speckled sky
when she is not there, when memory only
      lifts her above the horizon, pulls her
above me where I lie and wait.

If I loved the earth at twilight
when mountains are soft contours in the dying light,
when the lake lies silver and still and I wade deeper,
      beyond the shallows until
I am buoyed, afloat and surrounded by her touch,
I would not call her a woman.

Oh no, each thing I praised I would be sure to say
was only what it was, was not what my body
most desired, the other half of my torn self,
was not what I need most when my spirit
wishes to speak without words.

I would say nothing to the woman I loved,
not even in what I write because I would not
      have others know how she is all
they could want, would not want even
the smallest syllable to lie between us.

SERENADE FOR A FLIRT

If Botticelli painted you, he'd die
or hang up all his brushes, take to drink.
What would be left for his palette once he'd seen
such slender hips, mauve eyes, and bow-like lips?
I guess he could have spent the rest of his days
in filling the spaces, flower by delicate flower,
sketching rabbits or larks in elegant trees,
a unicorn or two in languid poses.

I know how this can happen—once, you see,
I met a woman, loved and married her
(it wouldn't have mattered which event came first)—
making all other worlds peripheral.
Stars wheeled around us, flocks of birds flew south,
then north, then south with drab monotony
unlike our chameleon world of rainbow changes.
A child played at our feet, then grew so large
he had to find his own world to inhabit.

For moments when you walked into the room
you snatched my breath away, you made me think
that I could write a poem to you, not her.
But love sings variations on a theme
not concealed beneath appoggiaturas.
This poem, dear maiden in your silken dress,
is not about you after all. I sing
the same old song that she and our love renew.

LANDFALL

*. . . we found shoal water, which smelt so sweetly and was so strong a
smell as if we had been in the midst of some delicate garden abounding
with all kind of odoriferous flowers, by which we were assured that
land could not be far distant.*
First Voyage Made to Virginia, 1584

Even June 21st is a night too long.
I wake in dark certain when light begins
its slow wash up the walls, the tide turning
but leaving behind relentless stains of black
on the shore of our room, I'll will myself to touch
those other pillows that no weight has formed,
and this will be the way each morning comes
on the voyage across what time remains for me.

Lying in the wake of that dream I do not dare
to reach toward the place where you should lie.
What if that night I dread has already come,
what if I'd lain down beside you in make-believe,
nearly sleeping, determined the end was only
of another day when lulled in doldrums of habit
I'd scrubbed the decks of my daily life, listened
to the hesitant wind in luff and billow of trees?

But flapping curtains reassure me. Nothing
so sure as an open window, passage at last
into summer coming so late could ever betray us.
The odor of lilacs and first sweet lilies of the valley
wash over us as I turn to touch your wrist,
its slow and sleeping pulse that lets me know
we've beached on another undiscovered day.

ANNIVERSARY

Does guilt always come to visit love
from time to time, bearing black roses,
standing on the threshold and asking permission
to enter? I have been faithful to you since
the first afternoon we lay together on your bed,
even though another woman was my wife.
Then why do I smell sometimes that perfume
of rot, hear the visitor shuffling his feet?
I confess to many things time revealed,
slow seepage of light like a prolonged dawn.

I see how love then lacked the urgency of age,
how I mistook the quick flash of our nights
for what was more truly there, pervasive
as if the scent of lilacs in a distant yard
was brought to us as we slept by breezes
through an open window. I see how bodies
we thought would endure forever disguised
ones that have shifted in shape, different
as parents are from their children.

I see that the things we did not say, forgot
to speak, were what we were really trying
to express, and now, so silenced by our love,
we need not utter. I would turn to the figure
at the door, seize his shadowy petals
and bring them to you asking forgiveness,
but I know there is no room in any vase
in our house for anything but blossoms
that gather light from unshuttered windows,
fill the many rooms we have built with
fragrance of memories we could not
have imagined then, having in those days
only an ignorance of time.

THE RETURN OF THE STRANGERS

Years ago we thought it naturally so easy
to spread and thrust and gibber out
whatever the mouth could form in ecstasy.
Then came a muting of desire, a falling off
of lust and easy joy. The old bed creaked
to insomniac turns, the limbs lay flat
or tightly curled, and when the clock
buzzed off to say *wake up*, we cursed it
for redundancy. Was it kids, sleeping
one room away who seemed to lie
between us like a naked sword forbidding
all foreplay, admitting only a furtive poke
and moan until dawn rasped across the roof
and duties rattled up against our door?
We could have kept our bodies cold,
marmoreal nakedness making our lives
into medicinal specialties the way
a gynecologist sees only names of parts
and never the flower unfolding petaled lips.

But one summer night, after we'd packed
the last child into college, as if we'd heard
some satyr in a wood blowing his horn,
the answering dryad's song, we saw
in the sultry lightning's flash a breast,
a rising prick, hips curved ready to let
the coiled years go. *Whose voice
was that?* we thought after the act
was played out like the storm, after
the slap of bed slats and pounding rain
grew still. All those years we'd talked
or yelled in dreams but hadn't used
the notes that only abandoned love

can sing. And so we lay there
in the dark again, lost in the woods
we thought we knew by heart.

A MOMENTARY STAY

I push away the bills,
lift a book. No, it's time
to meet someone at an office
down the road, or am I
the one to pick up our boy
in another hour? The car
smells of a leak. The CD player
is jammed, the street is blocked,
and I am shunted miles away
from where I want to go.
Across bright air a fire engine
wails. Coming? In retreat? Pray
for those at its destination.

Too little water in the pan.
Burnt asparagus for dinner.
Someone calls to sell me stocks
just as the wine begins to erase
the knowledge of my debts.
By ten o'clock I walk the house
alone, settle into a chair
near windows, in the dark.

Imagine arclights in Rome
lifting the Pantheon from its square,
sambuca savored after dinner
as obsequious waiters hover.
But I'm too old to believe
in buying what I want.

Lean past the sash. Lilacs bloom
to fill each breath, stars made faint
by complicated streets still shine.

So lock the doors, lights out.
Accept the hazard of dreams
that purge so we can wake
to one moment when we are
neither here nor there.

THE GARDEN

I must have walked with him
one evening after dinner, my hand
in his, across the road to the plot
we called a 'victory garden.' I thought
by growing tomatoes, beans, some kale,
we'd bring all war to end, but didn't know
what war was anyway, except for shades
we put on windows to prevent our lights
from shining into night. Even then
I didn't believe in bombs, preferred
to raise the shades so I could lie and watch
the moon on sleepless nights move on.
I smell rank loam he turned at dusk,
I sense his stooping form as he opened
an envelope of peas. *Come on, carefully,*
one by one. I lifted each pale eye,
set it in soil where for a while
it stared like a distant star, and then
we covered them with earth,
tucked them in with our palms
to let them have their dreams
as I have this—my father living
as I thought he always would.

MY FATHER, DYING

In the moment when pain ceased,
as darkness more dark than any night you had seen
rolled toward you and you held your breath
as if you might survive some ocean breaker
flinging you high on another shore,
was memory there also?
What came in that stillness
where the dark wave had no sound
and you were no longer breathing, your blood
held perfectly still too in that dark?

When you were a small boy and roamed
beyond your father's fields, a collie
walked with you, nosing the burrows of moles
and groundhogs, flushing birds from their nests.
When you came home from college, you heaved
bails onto wagons, clucked the horses forward,
then slung load after load into hayricks
and lofts. When your father died,
you were far from home where the dogs
of Anatolia barked at your figure searching
rocky hills for signs of ancient Rome.
Did a line of dusky trees, grass and sundial
come back to you and also the touch of a hand
in yours, your future wife's, the pale face
she pressed to your collar bone?

Does memory surge at all against
the indifferent silence, black wave that holds
neither pain nor loss of pain, joy nor listless heat
of long afternoons? The body exhales, rough heart
stops beating. We burn what remains
and drop the urn into busy soil.

Old father, does greeny air of new-mown hay,
the dog's cold nose nudging your leg
remain strong enough for one last return?
Will I see you at my end?

Over your ashes I have piled stones.
After a rainfall, under the sun, they gleam.

PARTIAL CORRESPONDENCE

First day of spring, but clouds spit snow
toward a half-thawed ground, geese
fly north in ragged wedges, wheel,
can't decide where to land. I imagine
you in the blue chair behind me, hands
relaxed on your thighs. If you wish,
doze as you often did in old age,
waking to mutter lines of Virgil.

I'm reading the story of your life
you wrote at ninety, journey with you
from a farm through high-banked snow
to drafty, one-room school, on your way
to study the fate of Rome, to trace
the Braille of stone incisions naming
magistrates, tracking old provinces
from ruin to ruin in Anatolia, past wiles
of thieves and wild dogs as if charmed.
I too look down from mounds of forts
and see the legions toil to breech the walls.
When you name me I rise into these pages,
burden and love, ignorant of the portion
of your life I now reclaim by reading.

Each year I watch you survive to name
those who fall—parents, siblings, mentor,
the friend who raced you down a lodging's hall
and won. Always you walk just behind me,
hand on my shoulder. One summer I dug
the hole for your ashes, spade heavy
with rain-soaked clay, lowered the urn
while generations watched, then read
your epilogue: *the orchard father planted*

is old and most of it is gone. The line
of evergreens that once shaded a garden
has failed too, and most of the poplars that kept
the northwest wind away from the orchard
and house are dead and gone.

Whatever you have planted here lives on,
in March, in spring, in scattered snow
that melts even before it touches earth.

IN THE COUNTRY OF ABSENCE

My mother lives where hills don't echo
and roots of grass always sleep.
Birds spread wings but forget their use,
and benches in parks are stacked
ready for eternal winter.

My mother takes walks on paths
that are only a place to put her feet.
When sun shines through her window,
she opens her hand in light
and sees only a hand in light.

A teller at the Bank of Memory
warns, *Your account is overdrawn.*
At the station she sits with purse
in her lap waiting for the train
that has lost its way.

When she speaks without sound,
her lips are miming the distance.

BURIAL SPACE

1.

Midnight. We sleep on the porch because a breeze
can palliate heat, because we can hear the brook
and believe cool water circles its stones. You breathe
the even breaths of sleep. Coyotes howl
on some distant ridge, or is it a barred owl
hooting to its mate? I won't wake you to ask.

I have buried my mother today, casting her ashes
into the hole I dug beside the cairn
of my father's grave. When I buried him, first parent
to die, I had never rehearsed, did it in haste,
dropping the box and caching all his years
in glistening clay.

                    In the living room we hunched,
three generations trying to speak her on
through memory, reluctant to turn and view
the greenly shadowed glade. Words, as always,
brought us through till now—the silence, a distant
howl or hoot, screens sagging with the breeze.

2.

Because I cannot sleep, because I must face
the dark by myself despite its comforting sounds,
I float in the space of memory, free-falling
after the long day's orbit, and I am thinking
for the first time in fifty years of Laika,
space dog, Russian astronaut, alone
in the stratosphere after a cold November launch.
Female mongrel, stray caught on the streets

and, for her propensities, called 'Barker,'
she was trained to eat jellied food, chained
for hours to live in a capsule, never turning
for days at a time. But after launch they announced
Laika would not come home, no matter what.

For days we imagined a live beast doomed
to circle above us, eating her jelly, wondering
when her trainers would come. What does a dog
see in stars or blue-mottled circle of earth
familiar now to us, but new for the first
creature of earth to see us at such a distance?

Her death, they said, was painless, sooner than we knew
because they did not tell us for twenty years:
seven hours after the flight began
she quit her pesky barking, settled into
her elliptical gravesite that spun in silence through light
and dark more pure than any we knew then,
for two thousand five hundred and seventy orbits.
Cremated in her casket's final tumble,
she returned at last to the atmosphere of earth
in April where even the buds in cold Russia
or here in Adirondack woods were opening.
Her dust settled finely all over the globe
where we breathe her and she will pass from generation
to generation of exploring, expanding minds.
Paved the way for humans in space, they said.
Hard verb for light, mute dust, for knowledge she took
with her, untranslatable, she being merely
a dog. Painless the burning, blind the descent.

3.

A startled snort of deer, splash as it leaps
the brook. I think the mind has betrayed me again,
taking me to a place that denies me sleep
but is not the place I do not dare to enter.

When I opened the lid, inside was a plastic sack,
no different from the roll of storage bags in the kitchen,
and I untwisted the wire clasp, released
fine powder to crumbling soil. I did not retreat
from the dust that rose before I shoveled it under,
piled stone on stone to match my father's cairn.

Because I will not see her again except
in dreams where she will appear in many forms,
because I can do nothing about her fall
through light to the darkness of deepest sea and rock
or my own when the mystery of obliteration will be
so intimately mine that I will not know it,
I choose to drift slowly into sleep
listening to wind, the sound of a planet circling
on its axis around the fierce fires of origin.

HUNTER'S MOON

My father and mother are scattered across water,
and moon is so close my palm could touch it
as geese wedge their way to places
I will never go.

Why in this dawn do they fly without sound,
mute passage through wreckage of stars?

MAKING A MASK

I

Fourteen years ago I held you as you bawled
against the light of birth, first heave of lungs,
but put myself into your hands, born
into a wholly new life. Now on my back
I lie on the floor, you hover above my face,
applying wet strips of plaster to make
a mask for school. "How will I breathe?"
I ask as water drips across my ears,
alarmed how my lips will soon be sealed.
"Quiet," you murmur, "you'll ruin it." Still
as a coffined body, hands folded
on my chest, I try to stare at the ceiling
but can't resist watching your pursed lips,
frown of imagination trying to see
what you hope to make. "Close your eyes,"
you say as the strip descends. Straws
in my mouth, I am sealed, buried alive,
trying to believe you are still out there,
working in the light.

II

Nothing is left but the muffled scuff
as you pace, waiting for me to dry,
sludge shrinking while my face hardens,
skin pinched in the plaster grip. I trust
your shuffling near my stretched body,
the mutter as you order yourself.
Your fingers move gently on the edge,
testing the line between bare skin
and dead impression of my life.

What border have I slipped across,
and is your touch enough to bring me back?
In the tightening I feel my bones rise
through withering flesh, and I cannot suck
enough air through these straws, fear
how flesh is turning to parchment, hands
will never unclasp, our bronzed dog
will be clamped to my armored feet.

III

I remember how I would sneak
into the room where my father napped,
huge chest rising and falling slowly,
lips puffing in and out, to stand and hold
my breath for fear of waking the giant
I did not know because he was gone
beyond me now. Just tall enough
to reach his face, I held my fingers
close to his mouth, knowing even then
that if I ceased to feel air brushing
across the tips I should scream away
such sleep, should break the spell
that held us in the opaque and shrouded
afternoon, fearing the day when nothing
I could say would wake him.

IV

I sleep. The silence in my mind
when panic leaves is darkness of a cave
before some child with a torch lurches in

or falls to discover paintings on the wall,
naked men clad in skins of reindeer, heads
of buffaloes, and dancing as if they became
dead creatures they wore. If I come back
from this place you send me to,
will I ever be myself again, or will you,
as the aborigine fears, have captured
my soul in plaster, leaving me to wander
in the semblance of myself? Who was I?
Lying now in congealing darkness,
I slip down into that dream beyond
the stone or house or leafless tree we know,
as deep as space where it bends back
on its first explosion, beyond even that
to silence without a name. If some spirit
is in the mask, larval, ghost to be carried
with us day by day, then who looks out
through our own eyes, pretending to be?
The soul must have a place to rest, body
to identify when it returns each evening.

V

Done! you cry, plucking me back into light,
tearing the carapace of who I was
from my new-wet face. I stare at the ceiling
beyond you to sunlight dappling leaves
on plaster, kaleidoscopic shards the breeze
shifts into restless shapes. All color is gone
for a moment when I turn, blast of pure light
from the window, and I rise from the floor,
gasping as if I dove for leagues into

the cold detritus of eons. You laugh,
hold a mirror to show splotched white
in my hair, cheeks of a mannequin
powdered with a story I'd lived. I smile,
cracking the petrified skin, shattering
numbness, and you laugh again
as we see each other for the first time
in hours, trapped between dread and joy.

VI

All afternoon we paint the blank impression,
making my form into your creation, transforming
this death mask into a household god wild
with colors, and then, forming our own procession,
we prance raucously to your mother's study
and burst the silence of her thought, parading
the fierce countenance of a man I was
or might have been, holding above us
a fragment snatched from time, moving
so quickly from sound to moving sound.

for Nathaniel